Advance Pra

"This wonderful book cen_ and it is based on a true story. Details of this journey are beautifully written, and readers will easily relate to the themes of fear, friendship, kindness, courage, and trust. I also loved the emphasis on an awareness of the dangers present in nature, but also of natural protections and the concept that we are all part of nature! Young readers beginning to read chapter books will enjoy this book, but it will also serve as a superb read-aloud for readers of all ages, especially those who love animals!"

—RUTH A. OSWALD, PhD, Professor Emerita, Literacy Education Department of Curricular & Instructional Studies, The University of Akron

"*Sheldon's Journey* brings together elements which young readers love — a lost dog, a journey, friends, magic, and home — into a beautiful story which is sure to touch readers' hearts."

—ALICE B. MCGINTY, award-winning author of 50 children's books, including *Mushroom House Man: The Story of Earl A. Young and his Cottages of Stone* and *A Story for Small Bear*

"After writing the memoir, *River Love*, about her experience creating a forever home for a lost dog, Sheldon, Tricia Frey imagines what a dog might feel when looking for its family. Aimed for a younger audience, *Sheldon's Journey* sheds light on what we all feel when lost, afraid, lonely, mourning those we can no longer see, and even hopelessness. Sheldon is greeted by many creatures in nature on his journey and learns of his own inner strengths as well as the value of new friends whom he bravely asks for help. Once he finds his new 'one true home', he chooses to make room for both his old and new helpers in his new life. This tale is remarkable for its ability to reach readers on many levels and offers lessons on dealing with loss and recovery from it."

—MARY FAIRGRIEVE, Clinical Social Worker

Copyright 2022 © by Tricia Frey
All world rights reserved.

No part of this book may be reproduced, stored in a retrieval system, or transmitted in any form or by any means electronic, mechanical, photocopying, recording or otherwise, without the prior consent of the publisher.

Readers are encouraged to go to MissionPointPress.com to contact the author or to find information on how to buy this book in bulk at a discounted rate.

Published by Mission Point Press
2554 Chandler Rd.
Traverse City, MI 49696
(231) 421-9513
MissionPointPress.com

ISBN: 978-1-958363-26-3 (hardcover)
ISBN: 978-1-958363-27-0 (softcover)

Library of Congress Control Number: 2022915267

Printed in the United States of America

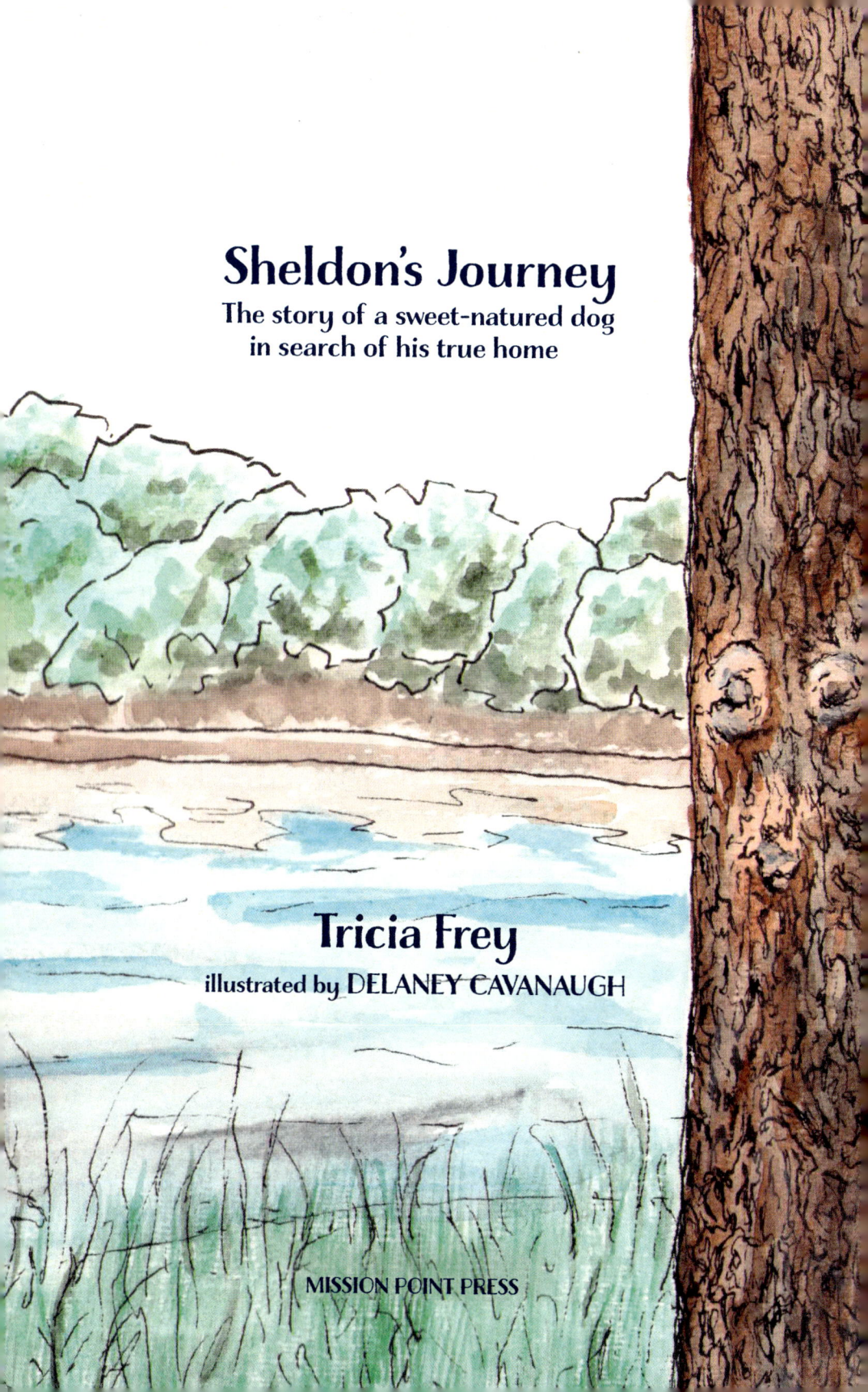
Sheldon's Journey
The story of a sweet-natured dog in search of his true home

Tricia Frey
illustrated by DELANEY CAVANAUGH

MISSION POINT PRESS

For Sheldon and Snickers

To: Beau & Linden —

Two sweet-natured children who love dogs. I'm happy to hear Mooch looks out for you. ♡

Enjoy the journey with Sheldon.

Lucia Frey

Author's Note

What you are about to read is based on a true story. Sheldon was a real dog. Snickers was a real cat. Both lived with me at Rivershire along the banks of the Boardman River in Traverse City, Michigan. *Sheldon's Journey* shares how I imagine Sheldon found his true home at Rivershire. He was lost, and when he arrived at Rivershire, he was timid and afraid of all people. For two years, Sheldon lived in a special house my sister and I made for him because he wouldn't come inside my home. We fed him and watched out for him. One very special day, October 11, 2008, Sheldon made the brave decision to come inside where Snickers and I welcomed him. At that point, we already loved him. We had room for more in the house made of wood and stone and we wanted to share it with Sheldon. While I don't know all the details of Sheldon's journey, I like to believe he had friends along the way, showing him the path. Actually, I'm sure of it. Nature has a way of guiding us to where we need to be.

Bravely go to that place where you are meant to be, dear readers.

With peace and gratitude,

Tricia Frey

Chapter 1
Sheldon's Journey Begins

In the cold, white wilderness walked a dog named Sheldon, a sweet-natured dog with one eye colored blue and one eye colored brown. He had thick white, black, and gray fur. In the fur on his right side was the shape of a heart.

Sheldon was all by himself and felt very alone. He wished he had a friend.

He heard no sounds; he saw no creatures of any kind.

Trees tall, strong, and bare were all around. With no leaves, there was no rustling, only quiet stillness.

"Am I alone?" asked Sheldon. "Am I lost? Where is my home?"

More stillness.

Sheldon began to wander over snow and through the trees. He didn't know what else to do.

"You are not alone," a voice said softly. The voice was welcome in the cold, white wilderness and Sheldon was not afraid.

"Who are you? Do you have a name?"

"Yes, it is Nibwaakaa."

Sheldon slowly sounded out the word. "Nib-WAH-kah. I like that name!"

"It is a word belonging to a native tribe of people," said Nibwaakaa. "It means 'to have wisdom.'"

"I cannot see you, Nibwaakaa. All I see are trees."

"Then you do see us, for we are the trees, all trees. We are connected through roots and branches, a community of life. You may call us all Nibwaakaa. We are here for you and for each other."

"Do you have wisdom, Nibwaakaa?"

"Yes, Sheldon, trees have wisdom. Trees are very wise, as you will see."

"You know my name! You must be wise."

"You, Sheldon, are on a special journey to your true home and we are here to help you find your way. We have been waiting for you. There is a path. Your home awaits."

Sheldon began looking at trees more closely. Knotholes in the bark of their trunks formed faces that peered at Sheldon. Sturdy branches appeared to be arms with long fingers pointing the way. Sheldon felt less alone. He had friends to help guide him.

And so, Sheldon began his journey on a rugged road lined on both sides with his new friends the trees. Sheldon walked and walked. Nibwaakaa did not speak and Sheldon wondered if he was alone again even though trees were all around him.

"Are you still here, Nibwaakaa?"

"Yes, Sheldon, always. Remember, we trees are all connected. Where there are trees, there is life. We are with you."

Sheldon was relieved to hear this. A journey is less scary with friends along the way.

"Sheldon, I suggest you rest," said Nibwaakaa. "You have a big day ahead of you tomorrow and night is falling."

These words concerned Sheldon. "Is night falling from the sky? Can it hurt me?"

"No, Sheldon. Night falls softly all around you, bringing cover and comfort. Night is a time for peaceful rest. Take yours now. You will need to be ready for tomorrow."

Atop the snow, Sheldon found a pile of dried leaves. It seemed like a very good spot for resting. At first, Sheldon could not sleep. The world was very quiet, but then, there was a rustling sound. Perhaps the wind? Another creature? If only there was some light like before when it was day. And night was colder than day. Sheldon began to feel cold and afraid.

Then, a glow. As clouds parted in the great night sky, a bright, round orb appeared. It cast soft light all around. Sheldon could see better and felt safer. "Who are you?" asked Sheldon.

"I am Moon. I am here to offer comfort to you at night. Sometimes, I am large and bright like tonight. Other times I am smaller, even just a sliver in the sky. And some nights, you will not see me at all, but I am here. I am always here."

"Are you my friend like Nibwaakaa?"

"Yes, I am your friend and will help guide you along your way. Like Nibwaakaa."

"Do you know Nibwaakaa?"

"Indeed, I do. We are all part of Nature. Now get your rest. There is much to do tomorrow and much more to learn. Sweet dreams, dear Sheldon."

"You know my name, too!"

"Ah, yes. I know you, Sheldon. And now, you know me. We will always be friends."

Sheldon fell into a deep sleep. Moon and Nibwaakaa were watching over him.

CHAPTER 2

Sheldon's New Friends

Sheldon awoke as a soft light graced the sky.

"Good morning, Sheldon," said Nibwaakaa. "Are you ready for today's journey?"

"I am rested and ready, but hungry," replied Sheldon. "I need to find food."

"Food will be provided, but you'll have to search for it. Begin your journey and trust that what you need, you will find."

And so, Sheldon moved down the path, trusting Nibwaakaa's words. As he did, another glowing orb, this one brighter than Moon, rose high in the sky.

"Who are you? Are you my friend?" The bright light felt like a friend, lighting the path, and making Sheldon's fur feel warm.

"Yes, Sheldon. I am Sun. I am your friend."

"You know my name too, just like Moon and Nibwaakaa."

"Of course. We've all been waiting to help with your journey."

Snow began falling softly from the sky. Sheldon thought to himself, "Just like night, snow falls too." At first, it came down softly, then more heavily. Soon, Sheldon could no longer see his new friend, Sun, through the thick snowfall. Sheldon was getting very hungry by now and felt a little frightened. He was getting colder, but he kept walking.

"Nibwaakaa, are you here?"

"Yes, Sheldon, remember, we are always with you."

Sheldon walked on. Snow began sticking to his fur and made his paws very cold. He wanted food and shelter. He wanted to stop. He wanted to rest.

"Keep trusting," he thought to himself. "Keep going."

And with that thought came a welcome sight. A house with a barn appeared through the snow. It was quiet and there seemed to be no one around. The barn door was open just a bit and Sheldon walked inside.

There, Sheldon found bales and bales of straw, plus some loose straw was scattered on the ground. "Ah, a warm bed," thought Sheldon. "I wonder if straw tastes good." Sheldon found out that it did not.

Suddenly, something darted across the barn floor, hiding behind the straw bales. "Who's there?" asked Sheldon. "Are you my friend?"

A furry face with big eyes and whiskers peered from behind the bales. "I'm Gwynn," came a purring voice. "I'm a cat and yes, I'm your friend."

Sheldon had never had a cat friend before. He had heard that dogs and cats don't always get along very well, but he was willing to give it a try with Gwynn. Sheldon felt he could use more friends to help with his journey.

"Are you hungry?" asked Gwynn.

Because he was so happy to find the barn and meet Gwynn, Sheldon had nearly forgotten how hungry he was. "Yes, I'm very hungry."

"Follow me," said Gwynn. And Sheldon did.

Together, Gwynn and Sheldon walked into another room in the barn. Sheldon could not believe what he was seeing! There was a large beast in a stall, making snorting and whinnying sounds. In the next stall, a smaller beast was prancing about, kicking up straw and dust, bleating in excitement. Both beasts seemed very happy to see Gwynn.

Thinking it the polite thing to do, Gwynn introduced Sheldon to her barnmates. "Sheldon, this is Dusty the Horse and Gus the Goat. They are very pleased to meet you."

"Indeed, we are," neighed Dusty.

"Really, really, really pleased to meet you," exclaimed Gus. Gus seemed to be excited about everything.

Gwynn explained to Sheldon that kind people owned the barn and took very good care of her, Dusty, and Gus by providing a warm place to live, fresh water, straw for beds, and plenty of food. Sheldon learned that he liked cat food. He also learned that straw made a soft, warm bed. Sheldon laid down with his new friends and fell fast asleep.

When Sheldon awoke the next morning, his friend Sun was shining brightly through the barn's windows. The snow had stopped falling.

Sheldon ate more cat food and took a long drink of water. Then he said to his new friends, "I must be going."

"No, no, no!" said Gus. "Please, please, please stay!" He was prancing a little more than usual, trying to convince Sheldon to stay.

"We would love to share our barn with you, Sheldon," said Dusty.

"It would be nice to have a dog around," said Gwynn, even though she was a cat.

"I would very much like to stay, but I must go," said Sheldon. "I'm on a journey to find my true home, and even though you are all so very nice to me, my true home isn't here. My true home is somewhere else."

"We will always remember you, Sheldon," said Gwynn.

"You will always be my friends," said Sheldon.

Gus stopped prancing. Dusty lowered his huge head. Both were sad to see Sheldon go.

Gwynn tried to make them all feel better. "Sheldon is right. He has somewhere special he needs to be, just like us. We are right where we are meant to be. Sheldon must also find his special place in this world."

And so, they said goodbye and Sheldon set off to find his true home.

CHAPTER 3

Someone Is Waiting

Not far from the barn where Sheldon had met his new friends, Gwynn, Dusty, and Gus, a cat named Snickers lived with her human, Twyla, along a beautiful river in a clearing called Rivershire.

They lived in a cozy house made of wood and stone. All around it were tall trees—pines, oaks, maples, and basswood. In the winter, snow covered the ground and frosted branches of the trees. Bits of ice sparkled at the river's edge. The river flowed swiftly—so swiftly it never froze.

Twyla and Snickers loved each other very much. Snickers often sat on Twyla's lap near the fireplace. Snickers had a coat of soft, thick, black and white fur and Twyla petted her over and over every day. They were very happy, but sometimes they felt alone even though they were together.

Twyla's heart was filled with love for animals of all kinds. She looked out her kitchen window every day and thought to herself, "We have room for more at Rivershire."

Snickers, curled up on her special soft cushion in the window seat, looked outside through the glass and thought about how nice it would be to have a furry companion to curl up beside her.

"I would like a friend," thought Snickers. "We have room for more at Rivershire."

One sunny afternoon, Twyla and Snickers were looking through the kitchen window at the same pine tree. It was a special tree because in its bark was a face looking back at them. Both Twyla and Snickers thought the face looked like a sweet-natured dog.

"Who is that?" thought Twyla. "Could it be a sweet-natured dog who wants to live with us?"

"Who is that?" thought Snickers. "Could it be my new friend?"

At that moment, they knew in their hearts that their wish would come true. Somewhere out there was a sweet-natured dog heading to Rivershire who wanted to live with them, too! This filled Twyla and Snickers with joy. And so, they watched and waited.

There was room for more in their home and in their hearts.

CHAPTER 4

River and Owl

Sheldon carried on through the woods. He looked up at the trees.

"Hello Nibwaakaa," he said. "I found some food, made new friends, and rested."

"That is good, Sheldon," said Nibwaakaa. "You searched and you trusted, and you found what you needed. Well done, Sheldon."

"I am ready to find my true home," said Sheldon.

And so, Sheldon walked on with Sun leading the way and Nibwaakaa's branches pointing in the right direction. He learned to find food in hidden places, sometimes by digging in the snow, sometimes in piles of discarded food scraps behind houses along the path. Occasionally, people saw him and felt compassion for him, so they put out bowls of food. When they weren't watching, Sheldon would sneak up and eat some. Sheldon was very timid around people.

At one point in his journey, Sheldon found another new friend.

As Sheldon walked along through the woods, he became very thirsty. Sheldon learned that in winter, the water in lakes, ponds, and puddles freezes. He ate snow, but it wasn't enough to quench his thirst. Sheldon kept walking.

"I have flowing water for you to drink," said a voice from among the trees.

"Nibwaakaa, is that you?" asked Sheldon.

"No, Sheldon," said Nibwaakaa. "It appears you have a new friend."

"Follow my voice, Sheldon, and you will find me," said Sheldon's new friend.

Sheldon walked in the direction of the voice and soon he heard a new sound, the sweet, burbling sound of flowing water. It sounded good to Sheldon's ears. He walked as fast as he could through the snow to meet his new friend.

Through the trees, Sheldon discovered water moving swiftly, clear and cool. He could see more trees and snow on the other side. The water had rocks both large and small in it. As the water washed over the rocks, it created the burbling sound Sheldon had heard and followed. He dipped his head carefully to the surface of the water and drank. The water tasted good and when Sheldon finished drinking, he asked, "Who are you, my new friend?"

"I am River. Stay by my side, Sheldon, and you will never be thirsty. I will help lead you home."

Once again, Sheldon trusted. He liked that he had many friends. He liked that they all knew his name.

Sheldon dipped his muzzle into River again for another drink. This time, he saw a face looking back at him! The face was also taking a drink of water from River.

"Who is in the water, River?" asked Sheldon. He was a little startled, although the face seemed friendly.

"That's just your reflection, Sheldon," said River. "That's what you look like."

Sheldon liked that he could see himself in River. He looked different than Gwynn the Cat and Dusty the Horse and Gus the Goat. He looked like Sheldon the Dog. He liked that. Friends could look different and still be friends.

Sheldon did as River said and stayed by River's side. River wound through the woods and Sheldon walked along beside. Nibwaakaa was there, too, and so were Sun by day and Moon by night.

Even though Sheldon had many friends helping to guide him on his journey, there were scary things too along the way. One evening, just as Sun was fading away and Sheldon was looking for a place to rest for the night, a large creature with massive wings and sharp talons appeared. It swooped down toward Sheldon, nearly snatching him up to carry into the sky. One of Nibwaakaa's branches shook in the wind, startling the creature and sending it away from Sheldon. Sheldon lay flat as he could in the snow.

"What was that?" cried Sheldon. He was very afraid.

"That was Owl," said Nibwaakaa.

"I don't think Owl is my friend," said Sheldon.

"Owl is a bird of prey," Nibwaakaa told Sheldon. "Owl hunts for rodents and other small animals to eat. Owl will need to find another meal tonight. Don't worry Sheldon, you have many friends watching over you."

Sheldon felt better and laid down to sleep for the night.

As Sheldon began to fall asleep, he heard a soft call in the night sky. "Who? Who? Who?" Sheldon's eyes opened. He listened very carefully. Again, Sheldon heard "Who? Who? Who?"

"I don't know who you are, but if you're wondering who I am, my name is Sheldon and I am a dog. Who are you?"

First, there was silence. Then came a voice from high in the trees.

"I am Owl."

Sheldon started to be afraid again, but instead, he decided to be brave.

"You scared me, Owl! Are you going to swoop down on me again? That was not very nice of you!"

"You are right, Sheldon. That was not very nice and I am sorry. Most owls stay awake all night long. I'll watch over you while you sleep. I would like to be your friend."

Sheldon considered this. He decided to trust once again.

"That would be very nice, Owl. I would like to be your friend, too."

Then, Sheldon fell asleep, and Owl watched over him all night long.

Chapter 5

Longing for Home

Sheldon awoke in the morning feeling rested and happy. He had another new friend, Owl.

Sheldon began to notice that Sun was out longer in the day and Moon spent less time in the sky at night. The snow was melting, and the air was warmer. "It's Spring," Nibwaakaa told Sheldon. "Winter has passed, and Spring is here." Sheldon didn't know exactly what Nibwaakaa meant, but he was sure he liked Spring. He wasn't so cold, and his paws and fur didn't have snow stuck to them.

Spring made Nibwaakaa's branches grow leaves. Flowers and mushrooms popped up from the ground. Sheldon loved these things, but Spring brought things that seemed scary, too.

One night, there was a big storm. Thunder was very loud and booming. Lightning streaked across the sky and cracked when it hit something. Wind blew hard, ruffling Sheldon's fur and making Nibwaakaa bend and sway. This upset Sheldon. He didn't want Nibwaakaa to fall down.

These things scared Sheldon, but he wanted to be brave.

Nibwaakaa tried to comfort Sheldon. "Wind, Thunder, and Lightning are all part of Nature, Sheldon. They can be scary, but they are also good." Sheldon was not so sure.

"Nature has a plan and sometimes there are parts of that plan that seem scary, but are necessary," said Nibwaakaa. "If you look at things in a different way, it might help. Lightning is beautiful, a colorful light show in the sky. Thunder is like a big, booming drum playing for everyone to hear. And when Wind blows through our branches and leaves, we start dancing. See, Sheldon, Nature is throwing a party!"

Sheldon thought a party sounded fun, so he tried to be brave when there was Thunder, Lightning, and Wind.

One day, after Sheldon had been walking a long time beside River and was starting to get tired, he began to wonder if he would ever find his true home. Sheldon wanted to stop walking. He wanted to be home.

"River, are you my home?" asked Sheldon. "Am I home now?"

"Sheldon, you have been on an important journey to your true home and you are nearing the end," said River. "I will never leave you. Like your other friends, I am a special part of both your journey and your true home, as you will soon see. We will always be together."

Sheldon felt happy when River told him this. He wanted to have his friends, but he also wanted to be home.

Sheldon laid down in the soft grass next to River. He would soon be home and wanted to be rested. River's sweet, burbling sound was like a lullaby and Sheldon drifted off to sleep. Moon, Nibwaakaa, and Owl watched over Sheldon as he slept. Sheldon felt safe. His friends were with him. Sun would wake him in the morning.

Chapter 6

Sheldon's True Home

Sun woke Sheldon early the next morning. "Sheldon, get up," said Sun. "This is a very important day."

Sheldon knew in his heart he would be home today.

And so, he walked. And he trusted.

Sheldon walked alongside River. Soon, they came to a clearing. All around it were tall trees—pines, oaks, maples, basswood—and colorful flowers bloomed. Mushrooms and toadstools popped up from the earth.

"You've arrived at a very special place," said River. "This place is called Rivershire."

In the clearing Sheldon saw a cozy house made of wood and stone. The windows glowed with warm light.

Sheldon looked about. He noticed the trees. Just like on his journey, these trees had knotholes in their bark that looked like faces. But here, in one tall, sturdy pine by River, the face in the tree was his! Sheldon saw his own face in Nibwaakaa!

Having seen his reflection in River, Sheldon knew what he looked like. Sheldon shouted happily, "That's me! *My* face is in that tree!"

Sheldon felt in his heart he had found his true home. But then, he wondered. What if there wasn't room for more in the house made of wood and stone?

Nibwaakaa reassured him.

"Welcome home, Sheldon," said Nibwaakaa. "The journey to your true home has ended. Someone has been waiting here for you all along. You are welcome here. You are wanted here. You are loved. Now, go ahead. Go up to the door."

Sheldon summoned up his courage and looked again at the house made of wood and stone. He looked at the windows that glowed with warm light. A woman was looking out one of the windows. There was a cat looking out, too! Their faces were filled with joy, almost as if they were expecting him.

Even though he still felt a little timid, Sheldon stepped up onto the porch of the house made of wood and stone. The front door opened, and in its frame stood the woman he had seen in the window. The cat was nearby, too, peering out at Sheldon from around the woman's legs. Sheldon hoped he and the cat would be friends.

"Come in, Sheldon," said the woman.

"You know my name!" Sheldon exclaimed.

"Yes," the woman explained, "Nibwaakaa and River told me your name just before you arrived. I am Twyla. This is Snickers. We have been waiting for you, Sheldon. We have room for more and are so happy you are here. Come inside."

Sheldon was very happy that there was room for more at Rivershire.

Before he stepped inside the house made of wood and stone, Sheldon looked back at Nibwaakaa.

"I will never forget what you and all my new friends did to help me," said Sheldon.

"Remember, Sheldon," said Nibwaakaa, "we will always be with you. We will always be friends."

"Yes," Sheldon agreed, "we will always be friends."

Then, Sheldon stepped inside.

He looked around inside the house made of wood and stone. It was cozy, warm, and welcoming. Twyla bent down and petted Sheldon's head. She looked into his eyes, one colored blue and one colored brown. She looked more closely at his face and saw it was the face of the sweet-natured dog in the bark of the pine tree outside her kitchen window.

Snickers rubbed up against Sheldon to let him know they were friends.

Sheldon felt he could be happy here. But something was pulling at his heart.

"Twyla," said Sheldon, "I am very happy to be here. It has been a long journey to find my true home. Along the way I've made some good friends who have been a special part of my journey. They have helped guide me here. I'm wondering … maybe I can stay on the porch for a while. It has a roof in case it rains and a chair with a soft cushion for a bed. I've gotten used to being outside and having my friends watch over me. Would that be okay with you and Snickers?"

"Of course, Sheldon," said Twyla. "We understand. We will be right here when you need us."

Sheldon was grateful that Twyla and Snickers understood and were being so kind. He now had friends inside and outside the house made of wood and stone. This made Sheldon feel happy and safe.

Twyla took a blanket and some food to the porch for Sheldon. After he ate, he jumped up onto the chair with the soft cushion where Twyla had put the blanket. It was the best bed Sheldon ever had. And though it was still daytime, Sheldon thought a nap sounded like a good idea.

"Sheldon," said Twyla before going back into the house made of wood and stone, "always know. You are welcome here. You are wanted here. You are loved. Sheldon, you are home!"

Sheldon (Photo: Susan Vants, Lil Red's Photography)

Tricia and Sheldon (Photo: William Sage)

Acknowledgements

Like Sheldon searching for his true home, writing and publishing a book is a journey, too. The following people made the journey much better and I am grateful.

To Delaney Cavanaugh, for their wonderful illustrations. One might say we met by chance, but it was pure kismet. From the start, Delaney grasped the feeling I wanted the images to convey, and beautifully and tenderly brought all the characters to life. That is a gift.

To Ruth Oswald, whose expertise and insight into the world of children's literature helped hone the narrative throughout many versions. Ruth was the first person to review and edit the manuscript and she did so with a keen eye and a loving heart. She is a truly beautiful person who I am blessed to know and call "friend."

To other early readers who were willing to bounce around ideas and offer valuable insight. They include Sandra Stegman, Mary Fairgrieve, Patricia Lanning, Delaney Cavanaugh, Jill Mann, and Ann Schrock Mooney. Their thoughts and comments helped shape the story and make it better. The conversations we shared along the way will always be special to me.

To the fine team at Mission Point Press—Heather Lee Shaw, Doug Weaver, Anne Stanton, and Darlene Short. Each makes the process of publishing as smooth as possible and their combined expertise in the varied aspects of publishing is mind-boggling. Heather—team leader and designer extraordinaire—always has the right answers (and patience!). Her design skills take every book she touches to a higher level. Doug and Anne read the early manuscript and provided spot-on editorial suggestions while offering invaluable support in many ways. Darlene is an expert proofreader and longtime dear friend. She makes my writing better every time we work together. They are all a joy to be around.

To young readers who have read this book and have a passion for reading and, perhaps, are writers and creators, too. Never stop reading, writing, creating art, playing music, whatever it is you are passionate about. It will not only enhance your life, it will make the world an even better place.

And finally …

To Sheldon and Snickers for being part of my life and Rivershire for drawing all of us to the house made of wood and stone along the beautiful Boardman River. It is a magical place, and I am grateful to call it home.

Snickers

Tricia Frey, author (Photo: Kathleen Partin)

About the Author

Tricia Frey was raised on a farm in northwest Ohio where her love of animals began. Over the years, pets in need of rescue—several cats and one wayward Sheltie named Sheldon—found their way into her home and heart. Early on, Tricia developed a love of reading and writing that she continued to pursue throughout her high school and college years, culminating in a Bachelor of Arts degree in Public Relations and Professional Writing from Capital University, Columbus, Ohio. Tricia has since made a career in sales and marketing. Her love of northern Michigan brought her to Traverse City in the late 1990s, where she now lives at her beloved Rivershire, nestled on the banks of the Boardman River. Tricia spends her free time nurturing her gardens, walking the many nearby beaches and hiking trails, and kayaking the beautiful Boardman. In 2020, Tricia published her first book, *River Love: The True Story of a Wayward Sheltie, a Woman, and a Magical Place Called Rivershire.* In *Sheldon's Journey,* young readers join Sheldon on his path as he searches for his true home.

Readers are encouraged to visit www.triciafrey.com to contact the author for speaking engagements or to get information on how to buy her books in bulk at a discounted rate.

*Felix and Tupperware,
representing Delaney Cavanaugh, illustrator*

About the Illustrator

Delaney Cavanaugh lives in northwest Ohio with their two cats, Felix and Tupperware. They work as a public school art educator and have a passion for teaching and art-making of all kinds. Delaney loves anything creative, including painting, papier-mâché, weaving, and metalworking. This is the first children's book they've illustrated.

Made in the USA
Middletown, DE
21 October 2022